# I Don't Wanna Share!
## It's Mine! It's Mine! It's Mine!

Jimmy Huston

Cosworth Publishing

All images are used under license from *Shutterstock.com*

Cosworth Publishing
21545 Yucatan Avenue
Woodland Hills CA 91364
*www.cosworthpublishing.com*

For information regarding permission,
please send an email to *office@cosworthpublishing.com*.

Dedicated to Me!
Just Me!
Me, Myself, and I!

Sharing is dumb.

That's okay. Most people don't want to share.

At least not at first.

You don't have to share.

Unless you want friends.

Think it over.

Does anyone ever share things with you?

Probably?

Certainly.

That's the way the world works.

We all share things with each other.

Including you.

When you hear a really funny joke, do you tell it to a
friend?

When you hear a new song that you like, do you tell anyone?

That's sharing.

You have a favorite toy, right?

Where did you get it? From someone?

How long have you had it?

You played with it a lot. Right?

Why would it matter if someone else played with it?

You'll get it back. It will still be yours.

Still don't want to share? Still think it's dumb?

Some little kids don't want to share.

Some big kids don't want to share.

Some boys don't want to share.

Some girls don't want to share.

You don't want to be the kid that everyone says doesn't like to share.

That's not the kid with lots of friends.

Maybe you've noticed that the other kids are having lots of fun—together.

Do you think people should share with you?

Maybe you don't—but...

...where do you get your meals?

Ever needed a ride?

Do you live by yourself?

Do you sometimes ask other people for things?

So you don't want to share? That happens.

Maybe this is the wrong book for you.

Just close the book until you want something from somebody.

Anything.

Even attention.

So go ahead. Close the book.

You're not in the mood to think about sharing.

Don't even turn the page. Just close the book.

You can come back later if you change your mind.

Maybe reading is not for you.

That's because a book shares information.

It's sharing thoughts with you (whether you want them or not).

In fact, those thoughts are shared with everyone who is reading this book or who has ever read this book or who ever will.

That's a lot of sharing.

So don't turn the page unless you're ready for sharing.

So you turned the page?

DId you keep reading or did you come back to the book?

Either way, that's good because you're thinking about sharing.

You are welcome here. Glad to have you.

Sharing starts early.

That's a good thing.

Parents share with kids.

That's important because there are lots of things kids can't do.

Kids can't cook.

Kids don't make good firefighters or cops.

Kids can't drive.

Kids aren't good astronauts either. Or doctors. Or judges.

Someday they might be, if someone shares knowledge and experience with them.

Remember, when you're sharing, it goes both ways. You share with someone, and someone shares with you. You'll get something back.

The easiest thing to share is a smile.

Try it.

Give someone a smile.

You'll get it back.

There are many different kinds of sharing.

We all share experiences.

We share playgrounds with others. That may mean taking turns on the swings or a slide, or you may just be running around—but you're sharing the yard.

An empty playground seems like a great thing, but after a few minutes, it feels lonely.

You can do anything you want, but there's no one to share the fun with.

Remember that sharing works both ways.

Taking turns is sharing, too.

You'll get your turn.

Everyone gets a turn.

That's sharing.

Maybe a little less of you, and a little more of someone else.

But it all evens out.

Ever been to a party?

Did you get invited back?

Parties are about sharing.

Ever had a party?

Did you want people to come?

That's sharing.

Do you dance by yourself?

Or do you dance with partners?

Sharing a dance can be lots of fun.

Do you like to sing with friends?

That's sharing out loud.

Do you have a dog or a cat? Or another pet?

How does your pet make you feel when you share time with it?

And, there is a special, personal kind of sharing for difficult moments when you don't want to be alone.

Sometimes it helps to share bad news.

When you feel bad, do you tell someone?

Being sick by yourself isn't good.

Your doctor shares knowledge about which medicines are best for each illness.

Your mom shares her knowledge of how much medicine to give you and when.

It's good to share work, too, even if it's just simple chores.

You can get help, or you can be a helper.

Have you ever been part of a team?

You share the action, the fun, and the work.

You share wins and losses.

We all share holidays. Even if we're not together, we have the same reasons to celebrate. We do many of the same activities, even if we're far away from one another.

We also share picnics, beaches, parades, parks, and more.

Teachers share all the things they know that you don't know yet.

That knowledge is going to come in handy.

Wait and see.

Carpools and buses are sharing, too.

Would you rather ride with others or walk by yourself?

We all share the same roads.

No one can afford their own personal highway.

So, we share the costs of building them, and then we share the roads.

We share books in libraries, entertainment in theaters, information on the internet, and knowledge in schools.

People on one side of the country are sharing the same things as people on the other side.

In times of trouble we share food, shelter, and medical aid.

Sometimes it's small, but sometimes a whole neighborhood needs help.

That's why we have police officers and firefighters and doctors and carpenters and ambulance drivers and cooks and teachers and clergy.

It helps to know that when we have emergencies, people we don't even know will help us—by sharing.

Lots of people share their time and their experience to help us when we need it.

There is personal sharing, with friends or family.

And, there is global sharing, with everyone.

We all are connected by the very same atmosphere.

We all breathe it, and it's where we get our weather—
and that means our water.

Those are two of the most important things we all
need for our bodies.

That's enough about sharing with the whole world.

We were talking about you.

Sharing is one of the ways you make friends. It's also one of the ways to keep friends.

Are you ready to share?

Start with a smile.

Then, if you want to share—prove it.

Share this book with someone.

**THE END**

## About the Author

Jimmy Huston is a native of Athens, Georgia, who lives in Woodland Hills, California with his wife and dog.

A recovering screenwriter and film-maker, he sincerely apologizes for all his silly books.

**Other odd children's books from Jimmy Huston**
*www.byjimmyhuston.com*

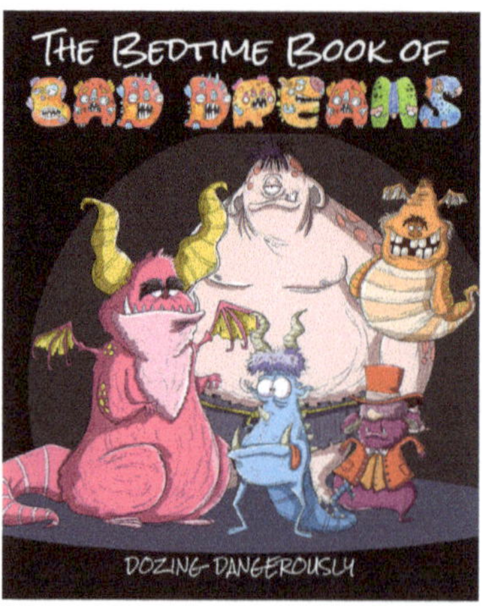

# Odd books about Neurodiversity

*www.cosworthpublishing.com*

(All available in Spanish.)

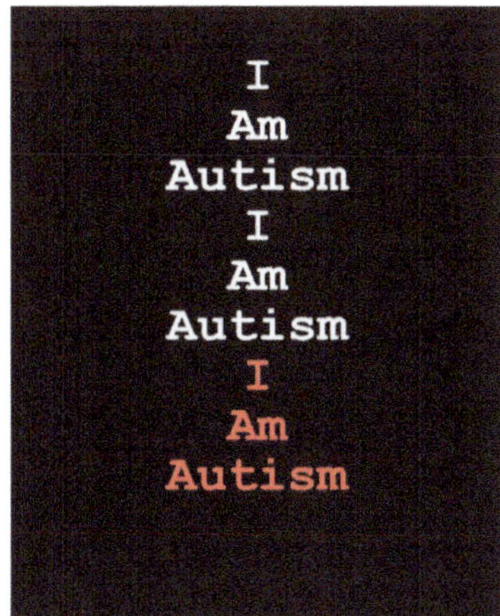


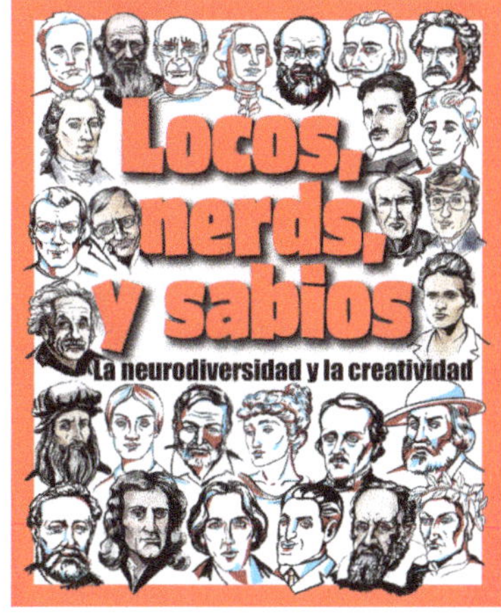

**Who* buys a book for a kid with dyslexia?**

Giving a self-help book to a dyslexic kid is like offering a drink of water to someone who is drowning.

So, have someone read it to you, so you can listen and think about it — and look at the pictures.

This book is also available as an audiobook. (You'll have to imagine the pictures.)

* Someone who cares.

# More books from Jimmy Huston
*www.cosworthpublishing.com*

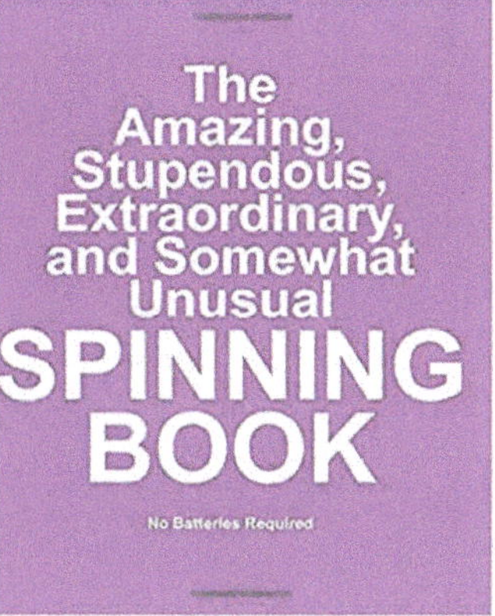

# Other books from Cosworth Publishing
### www.cosworthpublishing.com

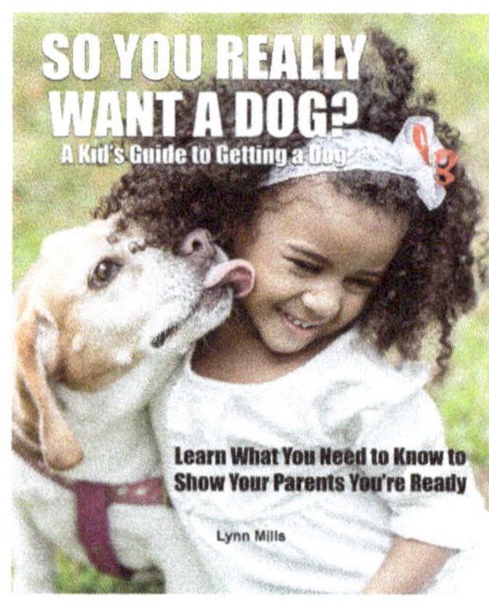

# Find it wherever good books are dreaded.

If you're reading this, you will not like this book. It's not for you.

This book is for all the people who are *not* reading this.

They won't like it either, but it's short.

They'll like that.

*"I didn't actually read this book. If I had, I would have loved it — but I never will."*                    Billy

*"Hate isn't a strong enough word for me. I loathe reading. I don't even like looking at pictures - which there are none of."*                    Wally

*"This isn't what I wrote about this stupid book."*
Zane

*"This is an excellent coffee table book, if your coffee table hates to read."*                    Solomon

*"This book made my teacher cry."*
David

*"My son loved this book. He said it was delicious."*
Mr. Jones

*"THIS BOOK IS SO DUMB THAT I COULD'VE WRITTEN IT."*                    Jimmy

# www.cosworthpublishing.com

**Thanks for buying, borrowing,
or swiping this book.**

At Cosworth Publishing we truly appreciate that,
and in return, we'd like to offer you one of our
E-books absolutely free—and worth every penny.

Just let us know that you want it, and we'll make
sure that you get it. Send an email to
*office@cosworthpublishing.com*.

Then, from time to time, we will
let you know via email when
we have a new book that you
might be interested in.

We won't do that very often
because we're basically pretty
lazy, and we don't produce
very many new books.

*Reviews are greatly appreciated.*

9 781965 153802